I AM Creating My Own Results Workbook

by
Barry Thomas Bechta

**UNCONDITIONAL
LOVE BOOKS**

*Redefining, Guiding, and Inspiring Humanity's
Connection to the Creative Power within.*

I AM Creating My Own Results Workbook
by
Barry Thomas Bechta

Library and Archives Canada Cataloguing in Publication

Bechta, Barry Thomas, 1968-
    I am creating my own results workbook / by Barry Thomas Bechta.

ISBN 978-0-9813485-6-8

    1. Self-realization--Problems, exercises, etc. I. Title.

BF637.S4B42 2011   158.1   C2011-904147-2

Publisher's Note
This publication is designed to provide accurate and authoritative information in regard to the subject matter covered. It is sold with the understanding that the author/publisher is not engaged in rendering psychological, legal, or other professional service. If advice or other assistance is required in those areas, the services of a competent professional should be sought.

Cover Image © 2011 by Zachary Rick Schroeder
www.lister96.deviantart.com

I AM
Creating My
Own Results
Workbook

Look for/See/Perceive bad in something
You will feel bad
Complain about something
You will feel bad
Think something is impossible
You will feel bad

Look for/See/Perceive good in something
You will feel good
Appreciate something
You will feel good
Think something is possible
You will feel good

All Pain and Pleasure is an inside job.
Your job!

Thoughts that feel bad lead to bad feeling experiences.
Forget them!

Thoughts that feel good lead to good feeling experiences.
Focus on them!

ACKNOWLEDGEMENTS

God

Binah

Anthony and Zach

Ellen and Clare

Melinda, Paul, Sydney, and Gryphon

Stephen, Margaret, Gabe, and Sam

Every person, place, and thing in my experience

The works of these Authors and Creators: Louise L. Hay, Prince, Iyanla Vanzant, Esther and Jerry Hicks with ABRAHAM, Richard Bach, Dr. Joe Vitale,, Dr. Wayne W. Dyer, Eckhart Tolle, Marianne Williamson, Jamie Sams, Dr. Norma J. Milanovich, Robert T. Kiyosaki, Alan Cohen, Mark Victor Hansen, John Randolph Price, Terry Cole-Whittaker, Michael J. Losier, Richard Paul Evans, Sandra Ponder, Robert G. Allen, Og Mandino, Shakti Gawain, Marc Allen, Lenedra J. Carroll, Anthony Robbins, Deepak Chopra, Pat O'Bryan, Paul Ferrini, Faye Mandell, Brock Tully, Helen Schucman & William Thetford, Gary Zukav, Neville Goddard, Jack Canfield, Tom Johnson, Neale Donald Walsch, Barbara Sher, Herman Hesse, **and Most Importantly You.**

INTRODUCTION

There are two questions that come up most often when I share my work with people. These questions usually have personal characteristics — my health, my relationship, my finances, my job — yet all these questions can be summed up in two basic forms:

How did I create my results?
How do I create my desired results?

Today, more than ever, we are hungry for specific knowledge — knowledge that helps us create what we personally desire.

Although, that knowledge can help us Create the specific results of ***Surviving*** — **food, clothing, and shelter** — many of us desire specific knowledge that encourages results of ***Thriving*** — **peace, well-being, and abundance** *(food, clothing, and shelter)*.

This book is designed to answer those two questions, so that you understand how you are where you are, understand how to clearly define your desired results, and understand how to create your own results of *Thriving* — all presented in a workbook format.

Remember you are the only one who is creating your results. Be as honest as possible about your results (don't sugar coat them) and you can go from wherever you are to wherever you desire to be. The more honesty you bring to the table of your life, the quicker you will manifest in your life the Results you desire.

Have fun as you work through this book. It is short and direct and can dramatically change the Results you are Creating. When you choose to believe with your entire heart, mind, and being that you can powerfully Create your Results as you Choose — you do exactly that!

I Love My Life!
Barry Thomas Bechta

TABLE OF CONTENTS

PART 1: Awareness of Your Current Results

PART 2: Your Vision of Your Desired Results

PART 3: What Results Do You Really Expect?

PART 4: Creation Vibration Activation

PART 1

Awareness of Your Current Results

□ Love   **Which Feelings did you feel this past week?**

□ Joy   Honestly check every feeling you felt.

□ **Freedom**

□ **Empowerment**

□ **Appreciation**   **Feeling Good is your**

□ **Eagerness**   **Path to EASE**

□ **Passion**   **Path to Good Feeling Results**

□ **Gratitude**   **Allowing Your Desired Results**

□ **Enthusiasm**

□ **Happiness**   □ _____

□ **Optimism**   *your word*

□ **Positive Expectation**

□ **Positive Belief**

□ **Hope**

□ frustration

□ pessimism

□ worry

□ righteousness

□ revenge

□ anger

□ pride

□ pain

□ outrage

□ unworthiness

□ discouragement   feeling bad is your

□ overwhelmed   path to dis-ease

□ shame   path to bad feeling results

□ jealousy   resisting your desired results

□ sadness

□ impatience   □ _____

□ hatred   *your word*

□ guilt

□ grief

□ helplessness

□ desperation

□ depression

□ despair

□ fear

□ beaten

Awareness of Your Current FEELING Results?

What emotional feeling word(s) would you use to describe the following areas of your life right now?

Physical: _____

Mental: _____

Emotional: _____

Spiritual: _____

Financial: _____

Time/Freedom: _____

Vocation/Career: _____

Intimate Relationships/Sex:_____

Family Relationships: _____

Community Relationships: _____

World Contribution: _____

These emotional feeling words you have written down represent the feeling Results of your life as either Good Feeling or Bad Feeling. You can change your Results. What SINGLE emotional feeling word would you use to describe your current life results?

Joyful?
Frustrated?
Enthusiastic?   _____
Impatient   *your emotional feeling word here*
                     from the list on the previous page

1

What current **Physical** Results (good or bad) have your attention today?

_____

What main **Thoughts** support your current **Physical** Results?

_____

What main **Feelings** support your current **Physical** Results?

_____

What main **Words** support your current **Physical** Results?

_____

What main **Actions** support your current **Physical** Results?

_____

What Are Your Current Physical Results?

How do you rate your current **Physical** Results 1 to 10?

1. Your lame results   10. You got game results

$$1 — 2 — 3 — 4 — 5 — 6 — 7 — 8 — 9 — 10$$

How would your most objective friend rate your results 1 to 10?

$$1 — 2 — 3 — 4 — 5 — 6 — 7 — 8 — 9 — 10$$

Do these ratings match? Where do you rate yourself now?

$$1 — 2 — 3 — 4 — 5 — 6 — 7 — 8 — 9 — 10$$

What short affirmative sentence do you use to describe your **Physical** Results on a daily basis?

eg: I'm fat. I love my body. I'm sick. I have a disease. I'm healthy and happy. I am a sexy god(dess).

_____

be completely honest with yourself

What is the reason you have your current **Physical** Results?

_____

_____

_____

What current **Mental** Results (good or bad) have your attention today?

_____

What main **Thoughts** support your current **Mental** Results?

_____

What main **Feelings** support your current **Mental** Results?

_____

What main **Words** support your current **Mental** Results?

_____

What main **Actions** support your current **Mental** Results?

_____

What Are Your Current Mental Results?

How do you rate your current **Mental** Results 1 to 10?

1. Your lame results   10. You got game results

$$1 — 2 — 3 — 4 — 5 — 6 — 7 — 8 — 9 — 10$$

How would your most objective friend rate your results 1 to 10?

$$1 — 2 — 3 — 4 — 5 — 6 — 7 — 8 — 9 — 10$$

Do these ratings match? Where do you rate yourself now?

$$1 — 2 — 3 — 4 — 5 — 6 — 7 — 8 — 9 — 10$$

What short affirmative sentence do you use to describe your **Mental** Results on a daily basis?

eg: I'm a genius. I'm stupid. I'm stuck. What is wrong with me? Things always work out for me.

_____
be completely honest with yourself

What is the reason you have your current **Mental** Results?

_____

_____

_____

What current **Emotional** Results (good or bad) have your attention today?

_____

What main **Thoughts** support your current **Emotional** Results?

_____

What main **Feelings** support your current **Emotional** Results?

_____

What main **Words** support your current **Emotional** Results?

_____

What main **Actions** support your current **Emotional** Results?

_____

What Are Your Current Emotional Results?

How do you rate your current **Emotional** Results 1 to 10?

1. Your lame results   10. You got game results

1 — 2 — 3 — 4 — 5 — 6 — 7 — 8 — 9 — 10

How would your most objective friend rate your results 1 to 10?

1 — 2 — 3 — 4 — 5 — 6 — 7 — 8 — 9 — 10

Do these ratings match? Where do you rate yourself now?

1 — 2 — 3 — 4 — 5 — 6 — 7 — 8 — 9 — 10

What short affirmative sentence do you use to describe your **Emotional** Results on a daily basis?

eg: I'm frustrated. I'm depressed. I'm worried. I'm jealous. I'm afraid. I'm loving. I'm appreciative.

_____

be completely honest with yourself

What is the reason you have your current **Emotional** Results?

_____

_____

_____

What current **Spiritual** Results (good or bad) have your attention today?

_____

What main **Thoughts** support your current **Spiritual** Results?

_____

What main **Feelings** support your current **Spiritual** Results?

_____

What main **Words** support your current **Spiritual** Results?

_____

What main **Actions** support your current **Spiritual** Results?

_____

What Are Your Current Spiritual Results?

How do you rate your current **Spiritual** Results 1 to 10?

1. Your lame results   10. You got game results

1 — 2 — 3 — 4 — 5 — 6 — 7 — 8 — 9 — 10

How would your most objective friend rate your results 1 to 10?

1 — 2 — 3 — 4 — 5 — 6 — 7 — 8 — 9 — 10

Do these ratings match? Where do you rate yourself now?

1 — 2 — 3 — 4 — 5 — 6 — 7 — 8 — 9 — 10

What short affirmative sentence do you use to describe your **Spiritual** Results on a daily basis?

eg: I love God. God is dead. God is good. The Universe is a Quantum Machine. The Earth Mother Provides for us.

_____
be completely honest with yourself

What is the reason you have your current **Spiritual** Results?

_____

_____

_____

What current **Financial** Results (good or bad) have your attention today?

_____

What main **Thoughts** support your current **Financial** Results?

_____

What main **Feelings** support your current **Financial** Results?

_____

What main **Words** support your current **Financial** Results?

_____

What main **Actions** support your current **Financial** Results?

_____

What Are Your Current Financial Results?

How do you rate your current **Financial** Results 1 to 10?

1. Your lame results   10. You got game results

1 — 2 — 3 — 4 — 5 — 6 — 7 — 8 — 9 — 10

How would your most objective friend rate your results 1 to 10?

1 — 2 — 3 — 4 — 5 — 6 — 7 — 8 — 9 — 10

Do these ratings match? Where do you rate yourself now?

1 — 2 — 3 — 4 — 5 — 6 — 7 — 8 — 9 — 10

What short affirmative sentence do you use to describe your **Financial** Results on a daily basis?

eg: I'm rich beyond my wildest dreams. I'm in debt. There's never enough. There is always enough. I AM Financially Free!

_____

be completely honest with yourself

What is the reason you have your current **Financial** Results?

_____

_____

_____

What current **Time/Freedom** Results (good or bad) have your attention today?

_____

What main **Thoughts** support your current **Time/Freedom** Results?

_____

What main **Feelings** support your current **Time/Freedom** Results?

_____

What main **Words** support your current **Time/Freedom** Results?

_____

What main **Actions** support your current **Time/Freedom** Results?

_____

What Are Your Current Time/Freedom Results?

How do you rate your current **Time/Freedom** Results 1 to 10?

1. Your lame results   10. You got game results

1 — 2 — 3 — 4 — 5 — 6 — 7 — 8 — 9 — 10

How would your most objective friend rate your results 1 to 10?

1 — 2 — 3 — 4 — 5 — 6 — 7 — 8 — 9 — 10

Do these ratings match? Where do you rate yourself now?

1 — 2 — 3 — 4 — 5 — 6 — 7 — 8 — 9 — 10

What short affirmative sentence do you use to describe your **Time/Freedom** Results on a daily basis?

eg: Everyday I take time for my dreams. There's never enough time. I work full time and take care of a family. I have time for me.

_____
be completely honest with yourself

What is the reason you have your current **Time/Freedom** Results?

_____

_____

_____

What current **Career/Vacation** Results (good or bad) have your attention today?

_____

What main **Thoughts** support your current **Career/Vacation** Results?

_____

What main **Feelings** support your current **Career/Vacation** Results?

_____

What main **Words** support your current **Career/Vacation** Results?

_____

What main **Actions** support your current **Career/Vacation** Results?

_____

What Are Your Current Career/Vacation Results?

How do you rate your current **Career/Vacation** Results 1 to 10?

1. Your lame results   10. You got game results

1 — 2 — 3 — 4 — 5 — 6 — 7 — 8 — 9 — 10

How would your most objective friend rate your results 1 to 10?

1 — 2 — 3 — 4 — 5 — 6 — 7 — 8 — 9 — 10

Do these ratings match? Where do you rate yourself now?

1 — 2 — 3 — 4 — 5 — 6 — 7 — 8 — 9 — 10

What short affirmative sentence do you use to describe your **Career/Vacation** Results on a daily basis?

eg: I love my job. I hate my job. I'm bored in my career. I'm stuck in my job. I rarely travel. I travel for work. I travel for fun.

_____

be completely honest with yourself

What is the reason you have your current **Career/Vacation** Results?

_____

_____

_____

What current **Intimate Relationship/Sex** Results (good or bad) have your attention today?

_____

What main **Thoughts** support your current **Intimate Relationship/Sex** Results?

_____

What main **Feelings** support your current **Intimate Relationship/Sex** Results?

_____

What main **Words** support your current **Intimate Relationship/Sex** Results?

_____

What main **Actions** support your current **Intimate Relationship/Sex** Results?

_____

What Are Your Current Intimate Relationship/Sex Results?

How do you rate your current **Intimate Relationship/Sex** Results 1 to 10?

1. Your lame results   10. You got game results

$$1 — 2 — 3 — 4 — 5 — 6 — 7 — 8 — 9 — 10$$

How would your most objective friend rate your results 1 to 10?

$$1 — 2 — 3 — 4 — 5 — 6 — 7 — 8 — 9 — 10$$

Do these ratings match? Where do you rate yourself now?

$$1 — 2 — 3 — 4 — 5 — 6 — 7 — 8 — 9 — 10$$

What short affirmative sentence do you use to describe your **Intimate Relationship/Sex** Results on a daily basis?

eg: I am a sexy god(dess)! I love my partner. I hate my partner. Things always work out for us. I am lucky in love. I am single.

_____

be completely honest with yourself

What is the reason you have your current **Intimate Relationship/Sex** Results?

_____

_____

_____

17

What current **Family Relationships** Results (good or bad) have your attention today?

_____

What main **Thoughts** support your current **Family Relationships** Results?

_____

What main **Feelings** supports your current **Family Relationships** Results?

_____

What main **Words** support your current **Family Relationships** Results?

_____

What main **Actions** support your current **Family Relationships** Results?

_____

What Are Your Current Family Relationships Results?

How do you rate your current **Family Relationships** Results 1 to 10?

1. Your lame results   10. You got game results

1 — 2 — 3 — 4 — 5 — 6 — 7 — 8 — 9 — 10

How would your most objective friend rate your results 1 to 10?

1 — 2 — 3 — 4 — 5 — 6 — 7 — 8 — 9 — 10

Do these ratings match? Where do you rate yourself now?

1 — 2 — 3 — 4 — 5 — 6 — 7 — 8 — 9 — 10

What short affirmative sentence do you use to describe your **Family Relationships** Results on a daily basis?

eg: I love my family. I don't know my family and they don't know me. My family members take advantage of me.

_____

be completely honest with yourself

What is the reason you have your current **Family Relationships** Results?

_____

_____

_____

What current **Community Relationships** Results (good or bad) have your attention today?

_____

What main **Thoughts** support your current **Community Relationships** Results?

_____

What main **Feelings** support your current **Community Relationships** Results?

_____

What main **Words** support your current **Community Relationships** Results?

_____

What main **Actions** support your current **Community Relationships** Results?

_____

What Are Your Current Community Relationships Results?

How do you rate your current **Community Relationships** Results 1 to 10?

1. Your lame results   10. You got game results

$$1 - 2 - 3 - 4 - 5 - 6 - 7 - 8 - 9 - 10$$

How would your most objective friend rate your results 1 to 10?

$$1 - 2 - 3 - 4 - 5 - 6 - 7 - 8 - 9 - 10$$

Do these ratings match? Where do you rate yourself now?

$$1 - 2 - 3 - 4 - 5 - 6 - 7 - 8 - 9 - 10$$

What short affirmative sentence do you use to describe your **Community Relationships** Results on a daily basis?

eg: I volunteer at the hospital. I donate money to worthy causes. I recycle. I smile when walking down the street. I do very little really.

_____

be completely honest with yourself

What is the reason you have your current **Community Relationships** Results?

_____

_____

_____

What current **World Contribution** Results (good or bad) have your attention today?

_____

What main **Thoughts** support your current **World Contribution** Results?

_____

What main **Feelings** support your current **World Contribution** Results?

_____

What main **Words** support your current **World Contribution** Results?

_____

What main **Actions** support your current **World Contribution** Results?

_____

What Are Your Current World Contribution Results?

How do you rate your current **World Contribution** Results 1 to 10?

1. Your lame results   10. You got game results

$$1 - 2 - 3 - 4 - 5 - 6 - 7 - 8 - 9 - 10$$

How would your most objective friend rate your results 1 to 10?

$$1 - 2 - 3 - 4 - 5 - 6 - 7 - 8 - 9 - 10$$

Do these ratings match? Where do you rate yourself now?

$$1 - 2 - 3 - 4 - 5 - 6 - 7 - 8 - 9 - 10$$

What short affirmative sentence do you use to describe your **World Contribution** Results on a daily basis?

eg: I don't do anything for the world. I think global and act local. Those are third world problems, not mine. I can make a difference.

_____

be completely honest with yourself

What is the reason you have your current **World Contribution** Results?

_____

_____

_____

When you are in your Heart/Feeling/Now, you let go and Let God/Life/Energy flow through you knowing that God/Life/Energy only shows you <u>your</u> very next step on <u>your</u> unique and personal journey.

Power of Now

Everything you create, everything you experience, you experience Right Now. Time/Past/Present/Future (T/P/P/F) are all experienced Right Now. Even the present moment, which you imagine is being experienced outside of you is always and only perceived within you.

Rarely from a Head/Thought/Time perspective is the description of *What Is* ever accurate. Most often in the human experience people think realistically about T/P/P/F. We look at *What Is* and we describe and judge *What Is* as realistically as possible. We are more concerned with describing and judging the forms of our experience accurately — even when the thoughts we use to describe and judge feel bad to us — "That is accurate." — we say to ourselves.

Simultaneously, our Heart/Feeling/Now perspective is concerned with Loving the people, places, things, and circumstances of *What Is*. When we are more concerned about describing and judging the forms of our experience in ways that feel good — even when our thoughts say these forms may feel bad — our life feels good.

Living the Heart/Feeling/Now perspective, we see everything present in our life as the next perfect step to our desires. Living the Heart/Feeling/Now perspective we Feel Relief Right Now about Time/Past/Present/Future.

When you Live in your Heart/Feeling/Now, you forget who you are/was/will be — you forget your likes and dislikes — you forget who you think you are supposed to be — you forget what you think should happen — you let go and Let God/Life/Energy flow through you knowing that God/Life/Energy only shows <u>your</u> very next step on <u>your</u> unique and personal journey.

The Power of Now is your ability to focus your Creative Power in ways that feel good right now (no matter what happens to you).

Think about what you like with good feeling expectation and you use the Law of Attraction to bring those very things into your experience.

Law of Attraction (LOA)

The Law of Attraction is the grand daddy of all Universal Laws. The LOA is the governing force in the Universe. The LOA states that like attracts like. Your powers at play within the LOA are your Thoughts, Feelings, Words, and Actions.

Like gravity, The LOA is always active. The LOA is consistently bringing you whatever you are a vibrational match to because your Thoughts, Feelings, Words, and Actions believe those very things.

You are a vibrational match to everything in your life. By looking at your life, you know what you are a match to by what has been Attracted to you?

If something is in your life — you attracted it with your Thoughts, Feelings, Words, and Actions.

Everyone attracts people, places, things, and experiences that match their creative energy — the LOA makes everyone right for their individual perspective.

Think about what you don't like with bad feeling expectation and you use the LOA to bring those very things into your experience.

Think about what you do like with good feeling expectation and you use the LOA to bring those very things into your experience.

> *"Whether you think you can or*
> *you think you can't,*
> *you are right."*
> *— Henry Ford —*

Thoughts

Feelings

Words

+ Actions

~~~~~~~~

= Results

4 Creative Powers

So how exactly do you attract the results you attract? You use your
4 Creative Powers to create your Results.

1. Thoughts	25%	**75% beliefs**	
		self worth	
2. Feelings	25%	**psychology**	
		motivation	
3. Words	25%	**Your Creation Vibration**	
4. Actions +	25%	25% mechanics	25% No Action
= Results	100%	100% results	100% No Results

1. Thoughts	25%	I can't do this.	I can do this.
2. Feelings	25%	I feel bad.	I feel good.
3. Words	25%	"This will never work"	"It's working"
4. Actions +	25%	I take lame action	I am confident
= Results	100%	lame results	game results

Life is set up for everyone to win.

Sometimes we win immediately because
we hold no resistence to our desires.

Sometimes we have to grow our
thoughts, feelings, words, and actions
to support our desires.

Creation Vibration
(75% of your results)

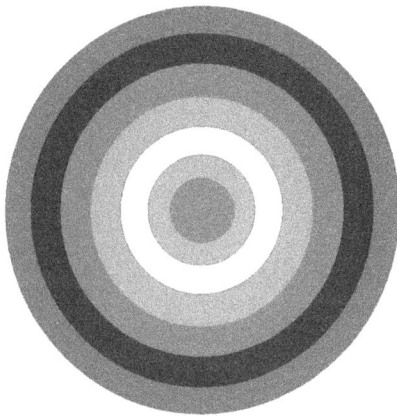

What are your results showing you believe in your heart?

Is your heart saying, "Give Me" or "I Give"?

Look at the people showing up in your life. Whatever those people are saying to you matches what is in your heart — *your creation vibration.*

Life is set up for everyone to win. Sometimes we win immediately because we hold no resistance to our desires. Sometimes we have to grow our thoughts, feelings, words, and actions to support our desires.

"I love my life!"

"Everything always works out for me."

"When I feel good everything works out for me."

"I find good feeling relief right now by my focus."

4 Actions Help
Make Time
Make Money
Make Resources
Make Connections

Successful People Appreciate
What Helps
Solutions
Realizations
Imaginations
Results
Possibilities
People

4 Excuses — 4 Actions

After listening to many people share the reasons they do not have what they desire, I have discovered that all the various things people use to stop themselves and to help themselves can be categorized under either the 4 Excuses or the 4 Actions.

● **4 Excuses Stop**	● **4 Actions Help**
● No Time	● Make Time
● No Money	● Make Money
● No Resources	● Make Resources
● No Connections	● Make Connections

Many people don't even make the conscious connection that they are the ones stopping themselves or helping themselves.

Unsuccessful People Complain about	**Successful People Appreciate**
● What sucks	● What helps
● Problems	● Solutions
● Reality	● Reality
● Manifestations	● Imaginations
● Results	● Results
● Obstacles	● Possibilities
● People	● People

All obstacles you experience you believe in.

If you did not believe in an apparent obstacle, you would not experience it because you would not even see it as an obstacle.

So ask yourself . . . How can I believe new effective beliefs? How can I believe in what is possible? How can I believe in the desires I imagine above anything else?

PART 2

Your Vision of Your Desired Results

"Success with all new ideas depends on how closely those new ideas already match your current beliefs."

~~Bill Bartmann ~~

How to Get the Results You Desire

There are two ways to get your desired results:

Do Things Differently
or
Do Different Things

Many people have tried both and found that they go back to doing the same old things once again — haven't you?

Bill Bartmann, author and businessman, who went from being homeless to becoming a billionaire says, *"Success with all new ideas depends on how closely those new ideas already match your current beliefs."*

That is the very reason that some people have success with a book, coach, workshop, or program, while some do not. The level of success with a particular idea or program depends on how much those ideas already match the person's current beliefs.

When people decide to do things differently or do different things, they often stop themselves because of fear. There are two types of fear:

1. Fear of harm: immediate bodily harm
2. Fear of the unknown: what we do not know

Fear of the unknown is the excuse that many people use to stop themselves when they decide to NOT do different things or NOT do things differently.

Fear: Feelings Eroding Away Reality

Faith: Feelings Automatically Inside a Truthful Heart

What **Physical** Results do you want?

_____

What main **Thoughts** support your desired **Physical** Results?

_____

What main **Feelings** support your desired **Physical** Results?

_____

What main **Words** support your desired **Physical** Results?

_____

What main **Actions** support your desired **Physical** Results?

_____

What Physical Results Do You Desire?

What short good feeling affirmative sentence could you use consciously to direct your **Physical** Results?

eg: I am open to my health and well being always feeling good.

_____

_____
imagine your new desire in good feeling ways

What is stopping your current **Physical** Results? Be open and honest about what Belief(s) come up when you say your short affirmative sentence. *All obstacles you ever experience are obstacles you believe in.*

_____

_____

What ideas allow you to have your **Physical** desires? All blessings you appreciate help you to have your desires — celebrate them when you see others having them, or you imagine having them.

_____

_____

What **Mental** Results do you want?

_____

What main **Thoughts** support your desired **Mental** Results?

_____

What main **Feelings** support your desired **Mental** Results?

_____

What main **Words** support your desired **Mental** Results?

_____

What main **Actions** support your desired **Mental** Results?

_____

What Mental Results Do You Desire?

What short good feeling affirmative sentence could you use consciously to direct your **Mental** Results?

eg: I am open to my thoughts taking me effectively to good feeling results.

_____

_____

imagine your new desire in good feeling ways

What is stopping your current **Mental** Results? Be open and honest about what Belief(s) come up when you say your short affirmative sentence. *All obstacles you ever experience are obstacles you believe in.*

_____

_____

What ideas allow you to have your **Mental** desires? All blessings you appreciate help you to have your desires — celebrate them when you see others having them, or you imagine having them.

_____

_____

What **Emotional** Results do you want?

_____

What main **Thoughts** support your desired **Emotional** Results?

_____

What main **Feelings** support your desired **Emotional** Results?

_____

What main **Words** support your desired **Emotional** Results?

_____

What main **Actions** support your desired **Emotional** Results?

_____

What Emotional Results Do You Desire?

What short good feeling affirmative sentence could you use consciously to direct your **Emotional** Results?

eg: I am open to feeling good on purpose in all circumstances and events.

_____

_____

imagine your new desire in good feeling ways

What is stopping your current **Emotional** Results? Be open and honest about what Belief(s) come up when you say your short affirmative sentence. *All obstacles you ever experience are obstacles you believe in.*

_____

_____

What ideas allow you to have your **Emotional** desires? All blessings you appreciate help you to have your desires — celebrate them when you see others having them, or you imagine having them.

_____

_____

What **Spiritual** Results do you want?

_____

What main **Thoughts** support your desired **Spiritual** Results?

_____

What main **Feelings** support your desired **Spiritual** Results?

_____

What main **Words** support your desired **Spiritual** Results?

_____

What main **Actions** support your desired **Spiritual** Results?

_____

What Spiritual Results Do You Desire?

What short good feeling affirmative sentence could you use consciously to direct your **Spiritual** Results?

eg: I Love God/Life/Energy joyously flowing through me.

_____

_____

imagine your new desire in good feeling ways

What is stopping your current **Spiritual** Results? Be open and honest about what Belief(s) come up when you say your short affirmative sentence. *All obstacles you ever experience are obstacles you believe in.*

_____

_____

What ideas allow you to have your **Spiritual** desires? All blessings you appreciate help you to have your desires — celebrate them when you see others having them, or you imagine having them.

_____

_____

What **Financial** Results do you want?

_____

What main **Thoughts** support your desired **Financial** Results?

_____

What main **Feelings** support your desired **Financial** Results?

_____

What main **Words** support your desired **Financial** Results?

_____

What main **Actions** support your desired **Financial** Results?

_____

What Financial Results Do You Desire?

What short good feeling affirmative sentence could you use consciously to direct your **Financial** Results?

eg: I open to good feeling abundance and money opportunities blessing my life with financial freedom easily.

_____

_____

imagine your new desire in good feeling ways

What is stopping your current **Financial** Results? Be open and honest about what Belief(s) come up when you say your short affirmative sentence. *All obstacles you ever experience are obstacles you believe in.*

_____

_____

What ideas allow you to have your **Financial** desires? All blessings you appreciate help you to have your desires — celebrate them when you see others having them, or you imagine having them.

_____

_____

What **Time/Freedom** Results do you want?

_____

What main **Thoughts** support your desired **Time/Freedom** Results?

_____

What main **Feelings** support your desired **Time/Freedom** Results?

_____

What main **Words** support your desired **Time/Freedom** Results?

_____

What main **Actions** support your desired **Time/Freedom** Results?

_____

What Time/Freedom Results Do You Desire?

What short good feeling affirmative sentence could you use consciously to direct your **Time/Freedom** Results?

eg: I enjoy more experiences of free time and freedom every day.

_____

_____

imagine your new desire in good feeling ways

What is stopping your current **Time/Freedom** Results? Be open and honest about what Belief(s) come up when you say your short affirmative sentence. *All obstacles you ever experience are obstacles you believe in.*

_____

_____

What ideas allow you to have your **Time/Freedom** desires? All blessings you appreciate help you to have your desires — celebrate them when you see others having them, or you imagine having them.

_____

_____

What **Career/Vacation** Results do you want?

_____

What main **Thoughts** support your desired **Career/Vacation** Results?

_____

What main **Feelings** support your desired **Career/Vacation** Results?

_____

What main **Words** support your desired **Career/Vacation** Results?

_____

What main **Actions** support your desired **Career/Vacation** Results?

_____

What Career/Vacation Results Do You Desire?

What short good feeling affirmative sentence could you use consciously to direct your **Career/Vacation** Results?

eg: I am open to my ideal career as a(n) _____.

_____

_____
imagine your new desire in good feeling ways

What is stopping your current **Career/Vacation** Results? Be open and honest about what Belief(s) come up when you say your short affirmative sentence. *All obstacles you ever experience are obstacles you believe in.*

_____

_____

What ideas allow you to have your **Career/Vacation** desires? All blessings you appreciate help you to have your desires — celebrate them when you see others having them, or you imagine having them.

_____

_____

What **Intimate Relationship/Sex** Results do you want?

_____

What main **Thoughts** support your desired **Intimate Relationship/Sex** Results?

_____

What main **Feelings** support your desired **Intimate Relationship/Sex** Results?

_____

What main **Words** support your desired **Intimate Relationship/Sex** Results?

_____

What main **Actions** support your desired **Intimate Relationship/Sex** Results?

_____

What Intimate Relationship/Sex Results Do You Desire?

What short good feeling affirmative sentence could you use consciously to direct your **Intimate Relationship/Sex** Results?

eg: I am open to my loving, nurturing, fun, and sexy relationship.

_____

_____

imagine your new desire in good feeling ways

What is stopping your current **Intimate Relationship/Sex** Results? Be open and honest about what Belief(s) come up when you say your short affirmative sentence. *All obstacles you ever experience are obstacles you believe in.*

_____

_____

What ideas allow you to have your **Intimate Relationship/Sex** desires? All blessings you appreciate help you to have your desires — celebrate them when you see others having them, or you imagine having them.

_____

_____

What **Family Relationship** Results do you want?

_____

What main **Thoughts** support your desired **Family Relationship** Results?

_____

What main **Feelings** support your desired **Family Relationship** Results?

_____

What main **Words** support your desired **Family Relationship** Results?

_____

What main **Actions** support your desired **Family Relationship** Results?

_____

What Family Relationship Results Do You Desire?

What short good feeling affirmative sentence could you use consciously to direct your **Family Relationship** Results?

eg: I am willing to experience my good feeling family relationships.

---

imagine your new desire in good feeling ways

What is stopping your current **Family Relationship** Results? Be open and honest about what Belief(s) come up when you say your short affirmative sentence. *All obstacles you ever experience are obstacles you believe in.*

What ideas allow you to have your **Family Relationship** desires? All blessings you appreciate help you to have your desires — celebrate them when you see others having them, or you imagine having them.

What **Community Relationship** Results do you want?

_____

What main **Thoughts** support your desired **Community Relationship** Results?

_____

What main **Feelings** support your desired **Community Relationship** Results?

_____

What main **Words** support your desired **Community Relationship** Results?

_____

What main **Actions** support your desired **Community Relationship** Results?

_____

What Community Relationship Results Do You Desire?

What short good feeling affirmative sentence could you use consciously to direct your **Community Relationship** Results?

eg: I love my good feeling community relationships.

_____

_____
imagine your new desire in good feeling ways

What is stopping your current **Community Relationship** Results? Be open and honest about what Belief(s) come up when you say your short affirmative sentence. *All obstacles you ever experience are obstacles you believe in.*

_____

_____

What ideas allow you to have your **Community Relationship** desires? All blessings you appreciate help you to have your desires — celebrate them when you see others having them, or you imagine having them.

_____

_____

What **World Contribution** Results do you want?

_____

What main **Thoughts** support your desired **World Contribution** Results?

_____

What main **Feelings** support your desired **World Contribution** Results?

_____

What main **Words** support your desired **World Contribution** Results?

_____

What main **Actions** support your desired **World Contribution** Results?

_____

What World Contribution Results Do You Desire?

What short good feeling affirmative sentence could you use consciously to direct your **World Contribution** Results?

eg: I am willing to manifest my good feeling world contribution.

_____

_____

imagine your new desire in good feeling ways

What is stopping your current **World Contribution** Results? Be open and honest about what Belief(s) come up when you say your short affirmative sentence. *All obstacles you ever experience are obstacles you believe in.*

_____

_____

What ideas allow you to have your **World Contribution** desires? All blessings you appreciate help you to have your desires — celebrate them when you see others having them, or you imagine having them.

_____

_____

You will always Feel Good when you
look at your desires with positive belief.

"I know I am going to get there."

You will always Feel Good when you look at
anything with a positive view -- appreciation --

"I love this result!
It leads me to a new possiblity."

Focus on Your Feelings More Than Forms

You will always Feel Bad when you look at your desires with negative belief. *"I don't see a way. This is impossible!"* You will always Feel Bad when you look at anything with a negative point of view — complaining — *"That result sucks! It's impossible"*

You will always Feel Good when you look at your desires with positive belief. *"I know I am going to get there."* You will always Feel Good when you look at anything with a positive view — appreciation — *"I love this result! It leads me to a new possiblity."*

ReaCtion — when you C what you desire after the fact, you are unconsciously creating — looking for the form evidence — feeling bad in the face of what appears. Often you react in the face of *What Is*. You are angry or blaming or complaining and feeling bad, without realizing that your power is in being able to C what you desire with appreciation. When you find yourself reacting and you catch yourself reacting and you redirect your focus — then you are consciously creating once again.

Creation — when you C what you desire first, you are Consciously Creating — when you look for the feeling evidence — when you feel good in the face of *What Is* (no matter what appears). You feel good, not because you are ignoring *What Is* (although you are essentially ignoring *What Is*). You feel good because you are focussing on the desire you want with positive expectation. You Feel Good because you are focussed on something expecting *What Is* possible. You feel good in the journey to your desires and the feeling journey is the way your life feels.

Stress (Feeling Bad) is related to ONLY 100% of illness.

Relief (Feeling Good) is related to ONLY 100% of Wellness.

What do you want to feel good believing right now?

Congruency of your Creative Powers

Are your results negative? Do your Results feel bad?

Negative Thoughts, Feelings, Words, and Actions are congruent. You always see the Results of congruent negative creative powers by the Results you get that feel bad to you.

Negative Creative Powers: Focus upon what you don't want. What you don't like. What isn't working. You regularly use the words — "Don't. Not. No. I can't. I wont. I hate this. This sucks!"

Are your results positive? Do your Results feel good?

Positive Thoughts, Feelings, Words, and Actions are Congruent. You always see the Results of your congruent positive creative powers by the Results you get that feel good to you.

Positive Creative Powers: Focus upon what you want. What you do like, What is working. What you appreciate. You regularly use the words — "Yes. I can. I choose. I am willing. I Love this. I feel this is the way."

What do you want to feel good believing right now?

All Results feel good or bad due to perspective, not due to a universal certainty. Another person in the same situation with a different perspective can turn a bad circumstance into a good one.

We all have done this.

We all can do this consciously too.

The One Degree of Connection that helps you experience anything in life is your ability to feel good.

One Degree of Connection to Everything You Desire

Have you heard about the Six Degrees of Separation?

Six degrees of separation refers to the idea that everyone on Earth is approximately six steps away from any other person, so that a chain of, "a friend of a friend" connections can be made, on average, to connect any two people in six steps or less.

Have you heard about the ONE Degree of Connection?

The One Degree of Connection that helps you experience anything in life is your ability to feel good. When you feel good, feel alignment, feel relief, and feel that your desire is already here, then you Feel Good already, which is the very reason you want everything you desire — you believe you will feel good having your desires.

Only when you feel that your desired results are already here do they appear.

To get to a place where you feel that your desires are already here, spend time daily Feeling Good in any way possible — **dance, sing, play, laugh, enjoy, run, tell good feeling stories, celebrate your matches, focus on thoughts that feel good to you.**

When you look away from your desires and you think you are not going to get there — you always feel bad.

When you look at your desires and you think you are going to get there (even without knowing how) you always feel good.

Care more about how you feel than what you want — then you become a vibrational match to what you want.

*Feeling Good is the one degree of connection
to everything you want.*

When you are ready, the universe can surprise and delight you beyond your imagination and expectation.

When you know that something is possible for you, then you often experience it soon after.

Your Job is Joy

Your Imagination + Your Expectation = Your Creation Vibration
Your Imagination + Your Expectation = Your Manifestation

If you feel your results are not here yet (doubt), you are giving more power through your imagination to what you do not have yet and LOA keeps your experience that way (ie: what you do not have).

If you feel your results are here (expectation), you are giving more power through your imagination to what you do want and LOA keeps your experience that way (ie: what you do want).

When you expect, trust, know, believe, appreciate, look for matches, see evidence of your desired results ready to happen — they will be around the next corner, in the next moment — because you feel they are about to happen. What you expect, the LOA unfolds in your experience.

When you are ready, the universe can surprise and delight you beyond your imagination and expectation. When you know that something is possible for you, then you often experience it soon after.

Your **MANIFESTATION** — always feels the way you expect, so expect your manifestation to feel good before it arrives and you feel good on the journey to every manifestation of your life. Feeling good on the journey is life.

Bad Feeling Result Worksheet

1. My current Result that feels bad is . . .

2. My feelings in the face of this situation right now are (identify your feelings, be honest, authentic, and non-judgmental) ☐ anger ☐ pain ☐ depression ☐ despair ☐ rage ☐ overwhelmed ☐ worry ☐ frustration ☐ pessimism ☐ discouragement ☐ revenge ☐ grief ☐ guilt ☐ unworthiness ☐ shame ☐ need ☐ sadness ☐ helplessness ☐ righteousness ☐ outrage ☐ impatience ☐ hatred ☐ fear ☐ pride ☐ jealousy ☐ desperation ☐ beaten ☐ longing ☐ other _____

3. I am willing to let my feelings be an indicator of the direction of my thought process. ☐ Willing ☐ Unwilling

4. I love knowing that the direction of my thoughts create my feelings. *I feel bad if I look towards my desires with negative expectation — complaining.* **I feel good if I look towards my desires with positive expectation — appreciation.** I love knowing that I control my feeling by the direction of my thoughts.
☐ I Know this is possible ☐ I Doubt this is possible

5. I love knowing that the direction of my thoughts create the framework of my experience. I love knowing that the people, places, things, and situations that present themselves — show my thought process — If I believe something is stopping me, my thoughts encourage that very thing to show up as I believe — as stopping me. ☐ I Believe this ☐ I doubt this

6. I love knowing that every Bad Feeling Result that presents itself in my life is a representation of my bad feeling thought process.
☐ Agree ☐ Disagree

Good Feelings Thoughts Transform My Results

1. I understand that every Result in life is neutral. Only when I think about a result do I activate my feelings. *If I look towards my result with negative expectation — complaining — I feel bad.* **If I look towards my result with positive expectation — appreciating — I feel good.**

2. The feelings I desire about this situation right now are ☐ Love ☐ Joy ☐ Freedom ☐ Empowerment ☐ Appreciation ☐ Eagerness ☐ Passion ☐ Gratitude ☐ Enthusiasm ☐ Happiness ☐ Optimism ☐ Positive Expectation ☐ Positive Belief ☐ Hope ☐ Bliss ☐ Peace ☐ Abundance ☐ Success ☐ Health ☐ Other _____

3. The good feeling (from the list above) that resonates with me the most about this situation is _____ .

4. I love knowing that the direction of my thoughts create my feelings. I love knowing that if I look towards my desires with _____ (#3), I support the good feeling result I desire.

5. My current results upon first glance felt bad. Now I know there is good in all my results when I look and find that. I now appreciate this (actually) neutral life experience by my focus upon the following positive good feeling aspects I now see in it . . .

PART 3

What Results Do You Really Expect?

You always get what you _really_ expect.

What if Your Results Feel Stuck?

Have you desired the same dream for years with little or no change in your manifestations?

Have you tried *everything* with slow Results?

Do your Results feel stuck?

If this is so . . . ask yourself what do you expect?

The way to know what you <u>really</u> expect about your results is by the actual Results you are getting.

You always get what you <u>really</u> expect.

If you have great **Physical** health, you expect great **Physical** health.

If you have poor **Financial** Results, you expect poor **Financial** Results.

Whatever you are experiencing as your Results . . . you expect and believe those are the Results you deserve.

Once you become Aware of what you expect Consciously (or unconsciously), because your Results show you what you really expect, then you can refocus your energy consciously to support your desired Results.

On the following pages, worksheets for becoming Aware of what you are expecting, and worksheets for what you desire to expect with some examples are presented.

Have fun working with these. They are designed to bring you Awareness of your creative power in action as shown by your current Results.

What You Really Expect About Your Physical Results Because Your Current <u>Negative</u> Results Are Showing Up That Way:

- I am 20 pounds over weight.
- I am tired daily.
- I get headaches.

_____

_____

_____

_____

_____

_____

_____

_____

_____

What Physical Results Do You Want to Expect With Your Positive Focus:

- I love having a healthy body weight for my height.
- I love having great energy daily.
- I love feeling relief daily.

_____

_____

_____

_____

_____

_____

_____

_____

_____

What You Really Expect About Your Mental Results Because Your Current <u>Negative</u> Results Are Showing Up That Way:

- I am flaky sometimes.
- I am not a genius by any stretch of the imagination.
- I rarely read books.

_____

_____

_____

_____

_____

_____

_____

_____

_____

What Mental Results Do You Want to Expect With Your <u>Positive</u> Focus:

- I love being focussed.
- I love having the right information when I need it.
- I love reading books I enjoy.

_____

_____

_____

_____

_____

_____

_____

_____

_____

_____

What You Really Expect About Your Emotional Results Because Your Current <u>Negative</u> Results Are Showing Up That Way:

- I am depressed.
- I am angry.
- I am worried.

_____

_____

_____

_____

_____

_____

_____

_____

What Emotional Results Do You Want to Expect With Your Positive Focus:

- I love feeling light and free.
- I love feeling in control.
- I love feeling confident.

_____

_____

_____

_____

_____

_____

_____

_____

_____

What You Really Expect About Your Spiritual Results Because Your Current <u>Negative</u> Results Are Showing Up That Way:

- I should meditate regularly.
- I wish I could believe in a good God.
- I hate going to a religious service.

_____

_____

_____

_____

_____

_____

_____

_____

**What Spiritual Results Do You Want to Expect With Your
Positive Focus:**

- I love feeling calm and relaxed moment to moment.
- I love feeling connected to Spirit.
- I love feeling comfortable wherever I am.

What You Really Expect About Your Financial Results Because Your Current <u>Negative</u> Results Are Showing Up That Way:

- I am in debt.
- I am struggling to make ends meet.
- I never have enough money.

_____

_____

_____

_____

_____

_____

_____

_____

_____

What Financial Results Do You Want to Expect With Your Positive Focus:

- I love being responsible for my money use.
- I love feeling more relief today about money.
- I love knowing that I always have enough money.

_____

_____

_____

_____

_____

_____

_____

_____

_____

_____

What You Really Expect About Your Time/Freedom Results Because Your Current <u>Negative</u> Results Are Showing Up That Way:

- I am overworked and underpaid.
- With work, and family, and friends, I have no time for me.
- I am stuck where I am. I can't see things ever changing.

_____

_____

_____

_____

_____

_____

_____

_____

What Time/Freedom Results Do You Want to Expect With Your <u>Positive</u> Focus:

- I love being paid extremely well doing things I love.
- I love having time for me and family and friends.
- I love feeling time freedom right now to do this exercise.

_____

_____

_____

_____

_____

_____

_____

_____

_____

What You Really Expect About Your Career/Vacation Results Because Your Current <u>Negative</u> Results Are Showing Up That Way:

- I am stuck making someone else rich.
- I am an artist, and artist's make very little money.
- The last major trip I took was over 10 years ago.

_____

_____

_____

_____

_____

_____

_____

_____

What Career/Vacation Results Do You Want to Expect With Your <u>Positive</u> Focus:

- I love taking 10% of my income to make my life better.
- I love knowing that some artists make millions of dollars.
- I love enjoying fun and sexy trips every year.

_____

_____

_____

_____

_____

_____

_____

_____

What You Really Expect About Your Intimate Relationship/Sex Results Because Your Current <u>Negative</u> Results Are Showing Up That Way:

- I am divorced and without any prospects of love.
- I rarely make love with my partner.
- I wish for more, but why do I have to change?

_____

_____

_____

_____

_____

_____

_____

_____

_____

What Intimate Relationship/Sex Results Do You Want to Expect With Your <u>Positive</u> Focus:

- I love being in love with myself in my relationship.
- I love making passionate love with my partner regularly.
- I love knowing that I create my results — I am willing to change.

_____

_____

_____

_____

_____

_____

_____

_____

_____

What You Really Expect About Your Family Relationship Results Because Your Current <u>Negative</u> Results Are Showing Up That Way:

- I fight with my siblings.
- I hardly talk with my parents.
- I hate some people in my family and they hate me.

_____

_____

_____

_____

_____

_____

_____

_____

What Family Relationship Results Do You Want to Expect With Your <u>Positive</u> Focus:

- I love feeling good enough that I get along with my siblings.
- I love having meaningful conversations with my parents.
- I love being able to let go of my past hurts and present hates.

_____

_____

_____

_____

_____

_____

_____

_____

_____

What You Really Expect About Your Community Relationship Results Because Your Current <u>Negative</u> Results Are Showing Up That Way:

- I see homeless people every where I go.
- I am tired of seeing negative media messages daily.
- I see miserable people every day.

_____

_____

_____

_____

_____

_____

_____

_____

What Community Relationship Results Do You Want to Expect With Your <u>Positive</u> Focus:

- I love being at peace about homeless people in my community.
- I love knowing I can direct my focus as I desire.
- I love seeing and appreciating great people in my community.

_____

_____

_____

_____

_____

_____

_____

_____

_____

What You Really Expect About Your World Relationship Results Because Your Current <u>Negative</u> Results Are Showing Up That Way:

- I see war and poverty and hatred around the world in the media.
- It is getting so expensive to travel around the world today.
- Why can't we all just get along?

_____

_____

_____

_____

_____

_____

_____

_____

What World Relationship Results Do You Want to Expect With Your <u>Positive</u> Focus:

- I love seeing peace and prosperity around the world.
- I love how affordable and easy travel around the world is today.
- I love feeling relief daily.

_____

_____

_____

_____

_____

_____

_____

_____

_____

What You Really Expect About Your _____ Results Because Your Current <u>Negative</u> Results Are Showing Up That Way:

- I see . . .
- I hate . . . .
- I fight . . .

_____

_____

_____

_____

_____

_____

_____

_____

What _____ Results Do You Want to Expect With Your <u>Positive</u> Focus:

- I love seeing . . .
- I love the way . . .
- I love feeling . . .

_____

_____

_____

_____

_____

_____

_____

_____

_____

PART 4

Creation Vibration Activation

You have already created what you desire through the experience of living your life . . . all of your work is about becoming a vibrational match to the desires you hold.

You are not asking for a perfect career, home, or relationship that is not now here.

You are realizing that your desires are already in your life and then they appear as if out of nowhere.

Daily Creation Vibration Activation Explanation

Your current Results in life always match your personal Creation Vibration (ie: your Thoughts + Feelings + Words) that you activate on a subject. Every subject you think and speak about has at its heart a particular *feeling* associated with it. You may think and speak about *the subject of money* but you can feel anywhere from *really bad about money* to *really good about money*.

The time it takes your desired manifestation to be fulfilled, is directly proportionate to the naturalness of your feeling of already being, doing, or having what you desire — think of something you already have in your life to understand your personal naturalness of feeling something is already in your life.

The secret of creating your desired Results in life lies in the *direction of your thoughts*. For example, right now as you read this book, you may be sitting or standing somewhere, and it would *not be natural* for you to run. However, you can easily *imagine yourself running* and while your consciousness is filled with your *imagined running*, you can forget that you are reading. In *naturalness of imagination* you could run into the ocean feeling the warm water slow your progress and *this would feel natural and real to you* — while only imagined in your mind.

Your desired *Results* can be achieved by *persistently imagining yourself being, doing, or having what you want to be, do, or have — FEELING YOUR RESULT AS REAL RIGHT NOW*.

Changes are not caused by *desiring something you do not have*, but by *feeling your desires are already here now*. Once you know and feel that what you desire is ALREADY HERE NOW, then it will be HERE NOW — *Do whatever you can to believe your desire is here now*.

Daily Creation Vibration Activation Worksheets encourage you to FEEL what is HERE NOW, not what is missing. When your desire is now here in feeling, it appears now here in form too. The more fun you have with this process, the more fun your Results become.

Daily Creation Vibration Activation SAMPLE Worksheet

> Right Now, I AM a Vibrational Match to my good feeling experience of . . . **Joy and Laugher and Peace and Ease.**
>
> **(Feel the ways your desire is here now,**
> *not the ways it is missing***)**

I write ten FEELING examples of my Faith, Belief, and Knowing my desire is already now here. The way to experience my desires is to FEEL UNITY and follow the path presented to me.

1. *Right now I easily laugh because I feel good*

2. *I love how I feel peaceful when I breathe deeply*

3. *I love feeling joyful about the birds in my yard today*

4. *I love the sun combined with rain in the form of a rainbow*

5. *I enjoy feeling relief wash through my body right now*

6. *I love drinking from this glass of cool refreshing water*

7. *I love remembering happy and peaceful memories*

8. *I love that my peaceful thoughts set up my peaceful life*

9. *I love the ease of activating good feeling creation vibrations*

10. *I love having the time to align with my good feeling desires*

Thank you God/Life/Energy for helping me activate my good feeling alignment with my DESIRE NOW HERE. These ten written feeling examples help me truly feel my *naturalness of feeling* NOW living what I desire to experience NOW. I do this activation daily knowing my Beliefs always Manifest.

I now have fun and leave today's manifestation details to God.

Daily Creation Vibration Activation Worksheet

Right Now, I AM a Vibrational Match to my good feeling experience of . . .

(Feel the ways your desire is here now,
not the ways it is missing)

I write ten FEELING examples of my Faith, Belief, and Knowing my desire is already now here. The way to experience my desires is to FEEL UNITY and follow the path presented to me.

1. _____

2. _____

3. _____

4. _____

5. _____

6. _____

7. _____

8. _____

9. _____

10. _____

Thank you God/Life/Energy for helping me activate my good feeling alignment with my DESIRE NOW HERE. These ten written feeling examples help me truly feel my *naturalness of feeling* NOW living what I desire to experience NOW. I do this activation daily knowing my Beliefs always Manifest.

I now have fun and leave today's manifestation details to God.

Daily Creation Vibration <u>Health</u> Activation Worksheet

Right Now, I AM a Vibrational Match to my good feeling experience of . . . *Radiant Health and Beauty and Well Being Blessing my life easily and joyfully right now. There are many examples of my Radiant Health and Beauty and Well Being in the following parts of my heart, mind, and being here now.*

I write ten FEELING examples of my Faith, Belief, and Knowing my desire is already now here. The way to experience my desires is to FEEL UNITY and follow the path presented to me.

1. _____

2. _____

3. _____

4. _____

5. _____

6. _____

7. _____

8. _____

9. _____

10. _____

Thank you God/Life/Energy for helping me activate my good feeling alignment with my DESIRE NOW HERE. These ten written feeling examples help me truly feel my *naturalness of feeling* NOW living what I desire to experience NOW. I do this activation daily knowing my Beliefs always Manifest.

I now have fun and leave today's manifestation details to God.

Daily Creation Vibration <u>Money</u> Activation Worksheet

> Right Now, I AM a Vibrational Match to my good feeling experience of . . . ***Money Blessing my life and feeling Financially Free to the tune of over \$_____ right now easily and joyfully and powerfully.***
> (Feel how your money desire is here now, *not how it is missing*)

I write ten FEELING examples of my Faith, Belief, and Knowing my desire is already now here. The way to experience my desires is to FEEL UNITY and follow the path presented to me.

1. _____

2. _____

3. _____

4. _____

5. _____

6. _____

7. _____

8. _____

9. _____

10. _____

Thank you God/Life/Energy for helping me activate my good feeling alignment with my DESIRE NOW HERE. These ten written feeling examples help me truly feel my *naturalness of feeling* NOW living what I desire to experience NOW. I do this activation daily knowing my Beliefs always Manifest.

I now have fun and leave today's manifestation details to God.

Daily Creation Vibration <u>Relationship</u> Activation Worksheet

Right Now, I AM a Vibrational Match to my good feeling experience of . . . *Relationship Blessing my life and Freeing me easily and joyfully and powerfully to love unconditionally.*
(Feel the ways your relationship desire is here now,
not the ways it is missing)

I write ten FEELING examples of my Faith, Belief, and Knowing my desire is already now here. The way to experience my desires is to FEEL UNITY and follow the path presented to me.

1. _____

2. _____

3. _____

4. _____

5. _____

6. _____

7. _____

8. _____

9. _____

10. _____

Thank you God/Life/Energy for helping me activate my good feeling alignment with my DESIRE NOW HERE. These ten written feeling examples help me truly feel my *naturalness of feeling* NOW living what I desire to experience NOW. I do this activation daily knowing my Beliefs always Manifest.

I now have fun and leave today's manifestation details to God.

Daily Creation Vibration <u>Career</u> Activation Worksheet

> Right Now, I AM a Vibrational Match to my good feeling experience of... *Career as a(n)* _____ *Blessing my life and feeling Financially Freeing to the tune of over $*_____ *right now easily and joyfully and powerfully.*
> (Feel how your Career desire is here now, *not how it is missing*)

I write ten FEELING examples of my Faith, Belief, and Knowing my desire is already now here. The way to experience my desires is to FEEL UNITY and follow the path presented to me.

1. _____

2. _____

3. _____

4. _____

5. _____

6. _____

7. _____

8. _____

9. _____

10. _____

Thank you God/Life/Energy for helping me activate my good feeling alignment with my DESIRE NOW HERE. These ten written feeling examples help me truly feel my *naturalness of feeling* NOW living what I desire to experience NOW. I do this activation daily knowing my Beliefs always Manifest.

I now have fun and leave today's manifestation details to God.

Daily Creation Vibration <u>Time/Freedom</u> Activation Worksheet

Right Now, I AM a Vibrational Match to my good feeling experience of . . . ***Time Freedom Blessing my life right now easily and joyfully and powerfully.***

(Feel how your time freedom is here now, *not how it is missing*)

I write ten FEELING examples of my Faith, Belief, and Knowing my desire is already now here. The way to experience my desires is to FEEL UNITY and follow the path presented to me.

1. _____

2. _____

3. _____

4. _____

5. _____

6. _____

7. _____

8. _____

9. _____

10. _____

Thank you God/Life/Energy for helping me activate my good feeling alignment with my DESIRE NOW HERE. These ten written feeling examples help me truly feel my *naturalness of feeling* NOW living what I desire to experience NOW. I do this activation daily knowing my Beliefs always Manifest.

I now have fun and leave today's manifestation details to God.

Daily Creation Vibration <u>World Contribution</u> Activation Sheet

> Right Now, I AM a Vibrational Match to my good feeling experience of . . . ***Contributing to the World right now easily and joyfully and powerfully.***
>
> (Feel the ways your world contribution is here now, *not the ways it is missing*)

I write ten FEELING examples of my Faith, Belief, and Knowing my desire is already now here. The way to experience my desires is to FEEL UNITY and follow the path presented to me.

1. _____

2. _____

3. _____

4. _____

5. _____

6. _____

7. _____

8. _____

9. _____

10. _____

Thank you God/Life/Energy for helping me activate my good feeling alignment with my DESIRE NOW HERE. These ten written feeling examples help me truly feel my *naturalness of feeling* NOW living what I desire to experience NOW. I do this activation daily knowing my Beliefs always Manifest.

I now have fun and leave today's manifestation details to God.

Daily Creation Vibration <u>God Is Here</u> Activation Worksheet

Right Now, I AM a Vibrational Match to my good feeling experience of . . . *God is here now. God Loves me now. God Blesses me now. God Cares for me now. God is Aware of me now. God focuses on the best for me now. God focuses on the best within me now. God performs this for absolutely everyone now.*

I write ten FEELING examples of my Faith, Belief, and Knowing my desire is already now here. The way to experience my desires is to FEEL UNITY and follow the path presented to me.

1. _____

2. _____

3. _____

4. _____

5. _____

6. _____

7. _____

8. _____

9. _____

10. _____

Thank you God/Life/Energy for helping me activate my good feeling alignment with my DESIRE NOW HERE. These ten written feeling examples help me truly feel my *naturalness of feeling* NOW living what I desire to experience NOW. I do this activation daily knowing my Beliefs always Manifest.

I now have fun and leave today's manifestation details to God.

Daily Creation Vibration <u>Well Being</u> Activation Worksheet

Right Now, I AM a Vibrational Match to my good feeling experiences of . . . *Love, Success, Abundance, Peace, Health, Joy, Freedom, Fun, Sex, Wealth, Relief, Relaxation, Kindness, Travel, Friendship, Generosity, Blessings, and any more wonderful well being good feeling surprises God/Life/Energy provides today.*

I write ten FEELING examples of my Faith, Belief, and Knowing my desire is already now here. The way to experience my desires is to FEEL UNITY and follow the path presented to me.

1. _____

2. _____

3. _____

4. _____

5. _____

6. _____

7. _____

8. _____

9. _____

10. _____

Thank you God/Life/Energy for helping me activate my good feeling alignment with my DESIRE NOW HERE. These ten written feeling examples help me truly feel my *naturalness of feeling* NOW living what I desire to experience NOW. I do this activation daily knowing my Beliefs always Manifest.

I now have fun and leave today's manifestation details to God.

How to know you are RESISTING the things you desire

- **FEEL BAD — frustrated, depression, hate, worry**
- **TIME FOCUS Passage of Time Past Present Future**
- **OUTER FOCUS on Objects on Something**
- Focus on People's opinions
- God Talks to everyone (feel bad and you do not hear)
- Life is a crap shoot and this is not your lucky day
- Unworthiness by others' standards
- Out-of-the-vortex (www.abraham-hicks.com)
- Hating *What Is*
- Complaining (needing attachment and control)
- Destroying self and others
- See hell being everywhere
- Obsessed with the worst feeling parts of everything
- Everything I want is No Where
- I am never a match to my desires
- Expectation with Doubt
- Effort with Frustration
- Focus on Feeling Bad Actions and Observations
- Misalignment with God and Self (inner), as well as people, places, and things (outer)
- Problem Orientated
- Prying Doors open
- Negative stuff annoys you
- Ineffectively focussed energy
- Stalled in life with a dying perspective
- Manifestations are an indication of misalignment
- When I feel unworthy, the Universe makes it so
- Agitated with needing something happen
- Anything attained can be lost
- Forms are your goals
- If you feel you don't have enough money right now, you never will
- If you feel your desire is missing, it always will be
- Action is more important than Alignment
- Your Perception of Bondage
- Struggle because LOA matches your perception of struggle

How to know you are ALLOWING the things you desire

- **FEEL G(OO)D — Peace, Joy, Love, Bliss, Confidence**
- **NOW FOCUS Timelessness Enjoying *What Is***
- **INNER FOCUS on Awareness on Nothing**
- Focus on God First
- God Talks to everyone (feel good and you do hear)
- Life is set up for everyone to win
- Worthiness by God's standards
- In-The-Vortex (www.abraham-hicks.com)
- Loving *What Is*
- Appreciating (without attachment or control)
- Encouraging self and others
- See well being everywhere
- Obsessed with the best feeling parts of everything
- Everything I want is Now Here
- I AM already a match to my desires
- Expectation with Belief
- Ease with Flow
- Focus on Feeling Good Actions and Observations
- Aligning with God and Self (inner), as well as people, places, and things (outer)
- Solution Orientated
- Praying Doors Open
- Negative stuff amuses you
- Effectively focussed energy
- Romping in life with a child's perspective
- Manifestations are an indication of alignment
- When I feel worthy, the Universe makes it so
- Peaceful without needing something to happen
- Nothingness attained can be lost and found again
- Feelings are your goals
- If you feel you have enough money right now, you always will
- If you feel your desire is here now, it always is
- Alignment is more important than Action
- Your Perception of Freedom
- Success because LOA matches your perception of success

When we are young, we make many different Choices.

As we grow older, we often limit the Choices we make.

Make more Choices until you get the Results
you desire and then you will have
all the Control available to you in your life.

You Can Control Your Choices

Each and every moment is a moment with Choice. Every moment you are making a Choice. Some Choices you make unconsciously, some Consciously; some Choices by default, some by Decision.

- You can Control your Choice of Thoughts.
- You can Control your Choice of Feelings.
- You can Control your Choice of Words.
- You can Control your Choice of Actions.

In life, there is only Choice and Experience of Choice. Ultimately, there is no wrong Choice. The idea of a right or wrong Choice only makes sense when you make one side correct and another side wrong. In doing so, you limit the possibilities available to you.

When we are young, we make many different Choices.

As we grow older, we often limit the Choices we make.

Make more Choices until you get the Results you desire and then you will have all the Control available to you in your life.

You control your Choices without ultimately controlling Results.

God/Life/Energy brings you the perfect Results in the forms of the people, places, things, and experience (right here right now) to help you accomplish your dreams — no matter what you may think to the contrary. If you are feeling bad when you see something, you are not thinking about the Result in a way that can benefit you.

From a human perspective, your Results can be unexpected.

From the Divine Perspective, your Results are Perfected.

Have more fun going to your Results and your Results will be more fun when you get there.

Your Results Are Always Up To YOU

Now that you have taken a deeper look at your Results (and your part in creating them) than ever before, what are you going to create?

You can be, do, and have anything you desire.

Sometimes your beliefs and expectations limit your ability to experience your Results.

Sometimes your beliefs and expectations allow you to immediately experience your Results.

No matter what, your Results are always up to YOU.

Life is set up for everyone to win.

Have more fun going to your Results and your Results will be more fun when you get there.

If you only read this book once, your Results are going to stay very similar.

If you use the concepts in this book every day until you get your desired Results, you will be a very conscious creator and you will be able to create anything you desire in your manifested experience.

You can do this!

Have fun doing this!

This is your life!

Make your life amazing!

Everything is possible until
one possibility is observed

Everything is possible until
you make a Choice

What do you Choose Now?

Newtonian or Quantum Physics as Your Creation Model

Most everything shared in this book is explained using the Newtonian Physics Creation Model of *Cause and Effect*.

Your Thoughts, Feelings, Words, and Actions <u>Cause</u> your Results

1. Thoughts	25%	**75% beliefs**	
		self worth	
2. Feelings	25%	**psychology**	
		motivation	
3. Words	25%	**Your Creation Vibration**	
4. Actions +	25%	25% mechanics	25% No Action
= Results	100%	100% results	100% No Results

That being said, we live in a world that is also blessed with the Quantum Physics Creation Model of *Everything is possible until one possibility is observed.*

Everything is possible until you make a choice.

You can Be, Do, or Have any experience you Choose.

What do you Choose Now?

What would absolutely be the most fun to Choose Right Now?

4 Levels of Manifestation

Level 1. Spiritual ➜ Inspired Results

Level 2. Mental ➜ Intended Results

Level 3. Emotional ➜ Instant Results

Level 4. Physical ➜ Incredible Results

4 Levels of Manifestation

Level 1. Spiritual: Inspired Results appear from the Spiritual Realms. Inspired ideas feel really good. No guess work is involved. Often inspired ideas appear to come out of left field. They often come through avenues wherein you have absolutely no training. Inspired ideas are the voice of God Giving Ongoing Direction saying, *"You can be, do, have, or experience something just for the fun of it."* Inspired ideas are the next logical step for you on your journey. Something just feels right — *Inspired* — have fun right here right now.

Level 2. Mental: Intended Results are formed after a period of conscious mental focus. First you are Aware you are in one place and then you desire to be in what you imagine would be an even better feeling place. This can involve any desire for a better feeling person, place, thing, or experience. Daily Creation Vibration Activation Worksheets are prefect for your conscious mental focus.

Level 3. Emotional: Instant Results You experience Instant Results every moment of your life through your feelings. When you think a thought it instantly manifests a feeling. Some feelings are really bad, some feelings are really good, while the majority of feelings appear nonexistent. Nonexistent feelings are feelings that you are no longer Consciously Aware of. We ignore our feelings so much through the years, that when we feel them — we are actually in a process of ignoring them. Awareness of your feelings in every moment is the Instant Results you desire because they Instantly tell you the way your Mental Results feel now and the way any Physical Results coming to you are going to feel. Your Feelings are God *Giving Ongoing Direction* in your life.

Level 4. Physical: Incredible Results fill your life experience right now. From this book you read, to your body, to your home, to your city, to your world. Your Incredible Physical Results always feel the way you believed they would before they even arrived. *Your Prior Feelings = How Present Forms Feel To You.*

Your Freedom Plan = Written Down Plan + Persistence

Freedom is attainable.

- Physical Freedom
- Mental Freedom
- Emotional Freedom
- Spiritual Freedom
- Financial Freedom
- Time Freedom
- Career/Vacation Freedom
- Intimate Relationship/Sex Freedom
- Family Relationship Freedom
- Community Relationship Freedom
- World Contribution Freedom

Too often people feel a lack of freedom because they have no written down plan.

Do you have a freedom plan written down?

Have you heard that people whom have written down plans attain their goals (and more) compared with people whom have no plan written down.

If you keep your ideas only in your head, daily mental distractions often supersede your imagined plans.

Your Freedom Plan = Written down Plan + Persistence

First, you have to write down your plan for all the Freedom areas of your life (see list above).

Second, you have to persistently stick to your plan, and then you will attain your defined level of freedom.

Let's use a simple example of Financial Freedom.

Financial Freedom = Written Down Financial Plan + Persistence

If you have a written down Financial Plan that states with every bit of money that comes your way 10% goes towards investments, and you persistently follow your plan, you have a much greater possibility of sticking to it and achieving the results you desire. Here are examples of this written down Financial Plan in action:

- Your Pay cheque comes in and you set 10% aside for investing.
- Birthday Money comes to you and you set 10% aside for investing.
- You find $10 on the ground and you set 10% aside for investing.
- You find $0.25 on the ground and you set 10% aside for investing.
- You have a monthly grocery budget and spend $50 less and you set 10% aside for investing.
- You have a monthly entertainment budget and a sale saves you $20 and you set 10% aside for investing.

If you have no written down Financial Plan . . . and you see something you want . . . you may buy it because you think you *need* it. Here are examples of no written down Financial Plan in action:

- Your pay cheque comes in and you spend it all and are short on money until your next pay cheque.
- Birthday Money comes to you and you spend it all.
- You find $10 on the ground and you spend it all.
- You find $0.25 on the ground and you spend it all.
- You have a monthly grocery budget and so many items are on sale that you get more food.
- You have a monthly entertainment budget and a sale allows you to buy more DVDs than usual.

Some people define Freedom with being able to do as they choose. Some people define Freedom with creating systems that ultimately free them in every area of their lives. There is no right of wrong way about how you define your Freedom. However, there are very different Results by the way you define and plan your Freedom.

In your life, you build muscles through the way you do things. Why not consciously build muscles that lead to your complete freedom.

Your Financial muscles are built by your daily Financial decisions. With the Financial Plan examples — one Written Down Financial Plan — one not written down, you get very different results.

If you have no written down Financial Plan and a bonus $10,000 comes you way, you will spend it all — because those are the muscles you have built.

If you have a Written down Financial Plan and a bonus $10,000 comes you way . . . you will set 10% aside for investing (perhaps more if your written down Financial Plan takes win falls into account) — because those are the muscles you have built.

Freedom is attainable.

What is your Written down Freedom Plan for the ten freedom areas of your life?

My Written Down Plans For This Year

I Plan to have Fun and Ease and Joy achieving my Plans in each area of my life this Year

Physical Plans For Year 1. Major _____ 2. Minor _____ 3. Dream _____	**Intimate Relationship/Sex Plans For Year** 1. Major _____ 2. Minor _____ 3. Dream _____
Mental Plans For Year 1. Major _____ 2. Minor _____ 3. Dream _____	**Time/Freedom Plans For Year** 1. Major _____ 2. Minor _____ 3. Dream _____
Emotional Plans For Year 1. Major _____ 2. Minor _____ 3. Dream _____	**Career/Vacation Plans For Year** 1. Major _____ 2. Minor _____ 3. Dream _____
Spiritual Plans For Year 1. Major _____ 2. Minor _____ 3. Dream _____	**Family Plans For Year** 1. Major _____ 2. Minor _____ 3. Dream _____
Financial Plans For Year 1. Major _____ 2. Minor _____ 3. Dream _____	**Community/World Plans For Year** 1. Major _____ 2. Minor _____ 3. Dream _____

Only 3 Plans are written down for the year in each area. 1. Major Plan (you do) 2. Minor Plan (you do) 3. Dream Plan (God does because you have no clue how to accomplish it)

My Written Down Plans For This Month/Week/Day

I Plan to have Fun and Ease and Joy achieving my Plans in each area of my life this Month/Week/Day with Focus and Fun.

This month's plans culled from my Year's Plan. I choose Plans that Fire me up with Excitement. 1. 2. 3. 4. 5. 6. 7. 8. 9. 10.	**Week 1 Plans** 1. 2. 3. God	**Monday** 1. 2. 3. **Tuesday** 1. 2. 3.
	Week 2 Plans 1. 2. 3. God	**Wednesday** 1. 2. 3. **Thursday** 1. 2. 3.
This month's plans for God to do for me because I have no clue how. 1. 2. 3. 4. 5. 6. 7. 8. 9. 10.	**Week 3 Plans** 1. 2. 3. God	**Friday** 1. 2. 3. **Saturday** 1. 2. 3.
	Week 4 Plans 1. 2. 3. God	**Sunday** Rejuvenate Plan Rejuvenate Myself G(oo)d Feeling Surprises

You Are <u>Both</u> the Teacher and the Student

Your Physical Results in life are your grades.

Your Thoughts indicate the direction you set for yourself.

Your Emotions indicate the way you feel about the direction you are setting in life with your thoughts — on a moment to moment basis.

Your Words indicate how your feel about the direction you have set for yourself. Are you complaining or appreciating more on a moment to moment basis?

Your Written Down Plans are the curriculum you set for yourself.

You are getting Results every moment of your life.

Your Results can be changed with focus.

Your home work is very simple — Focus Upon:

- Written Down Plans (Yearly/Monthly/Daily)
- Awareness of your Feelings (in every moment)
- Making Fun (a priority of every moment)
- Making Friends (or agree to disagree peacefully)
- Learning new Skills (for self directed tests)
- Asking for Help (from successful students/teachers)
- Taking more self directed tests (Action leads to Results)

You are going to get somewhere in life.

Set the direction of your life consciously and with fun and watch your life soar easily, joyfully, consistently.

Make Plans
Make Lists
Have Fun
Enjoy All Feelings
Make Friends
Learn Skills
Ask For Help

Have more fun by
taking more self directed tests
and enjoying your life soar

You are Creating
Your Own Results

Only You!

ABOUT THE AUTHOR

Barry Thomas Bechta is an artist, author, and film maker whose work centers around the concepts of Unconditional Love. Barry knew he wanted to write from a very young age and was encouraged with his artistic skills and only began writing full time in his thirties. He wrote his first book, *I AM Creating My Own Experience* as a personal journal to choose connection with God/Life/Energy. He has since written 17 inspirational books.

Barry loves to hear from people whom have connected with his writing and used it as a tool to improve their lives. If you would like to write him about your personal experiences as a result of reading any of his books, Barry encourages you to do so.

You can also get a Free Digital Copy of *I AM Creating My Own Experience - The Creation Vibration* from his main website:

www.unconditionallovebooks.com

Unconditional Love Books Titles of Related Interest
by Barry Thomas Bechta

I AM Creating My Own Experience
978-0-9813485-5-1
I AM Creating My Own Answers
978-0-9686835-1-4
I AM Creating My Own Dreams
978-0-9686835-2-1
I AM Creating My Own Relationships
978-0-9686835-3-8
I AM Creating My Own Abundance
978-0-9686835-4-5
I AM Creating My Own Success
978-0-9686835-5-2
I AM Creating My Own Happiness
978-0-9686835-6-9
I AM Creating My Own Experience - The Creation Vibration
978-0-9686835-7-6
I AM Creating My Own Experience - To Manifest Money
978-0-9686835-8-3
I AM Creating My Own Experience - 369 Conscious Days
978-0-9686835-9-0
Loving Oneness
978-0-9813485-0-6
Trust Life
978-0-9813485-1-3
I AM Creating My Own Financial Freedom - The Story
978-0-9813485-2-0
I AM Creating My Own Financial Freedom - The Lessons
978-0-9813485-3-7
Laughing Star's Guide to Laughter, Life, Love, and God
978-0-9813485-4-4

All of the above are books are available through your local
bookstore, or they may be ordered as digital downloads at
www.unconditionallovebooks.com

Barry Thomas Bechta is available for interviews, special events, workshops, and lectures that redefine, guide, and inspire everyone's connection to the Creative Power within themselves. To arrange author interviews, special events, workshops, or lectures, please contact:

UNCONDITIONAL
LOVE BOOKS

Unconditional Love Books
Box # 610 - 2527 Pine St.,
Vancouver, BC, Canada V6J 3E8

info@unconditionallovebooks.com

www.unconditionallovebooks.com

For additional copies of Barry's books, products, and services please contact your local book seller. Many products and services are Only available to order directly from the publisher as eProducts on the website.

Thanks for your purchase and Remember to Consciously Create your Life.

Right Now is the Only Moment of Creation

Enjoy it Fully!

www.ingramcontent.com/pod-product-compliance
Lightning Source LLC
Chambersburg PA
CBHW051831040426
42447CB00006B/471